The
Optimist's/
Pessimist's
Guide to the Millennium

Barbara Ann Kipfer, Ph.D.
and Ed Strnad

Developed by
The Philip Lief Group, Inc.

A Perigee Book

A Perigee Book
Published by The Berkley Publishing Group
200 Madison Avenue, New York, NY 10016

Published by arrangement with The Philip Lief Group, Inc.
6 West 20th Street, New York, NY 10011

First edition: February 1996

Published simultaneously in Canada.

Library of Congress Cataloging-in-Publication Data
Kipfer, Barbara Ann.
    The optimist's/pessimist's guide to the millennium / Barbara Ann Kipfer and Ed Strnad;
developed by the Philip Lief Group Inc. — 1st ed.
        p.   cm.
    "A Perigee book."
    ISBN 0-399-52191-7
    1. Twenty-first century—Humor. 2. Future—Humor. I. Strnad, Ed. II. Philip Lief Group.
III. Title.
PN6231.T76F56   1996
818'.5402—dc20

                                                                          95-23115
                                                                          CIP

Printed in the United States of America

10   9   8   7   6   5   4   3   2   1

Acknowledgments

The pessi-Mystic sooth-(nay)saying author gives his best wishes for the future to Brian Steinwand, Lidia Hasenauer, Christian Nagy, George Zarr, and JoAnn Strnad for their predictions. And to my son, Eddie, the future kid—may you read all this someday, and just smile.

—E.S. KGNJ65A@prodigy.com

To P.M., K.K., and K.M —B.A.K.

Introduction

"The future looks so bright, I gotta wear shades."—Barbara Ann Kipfer

"I have seen the future, and 'Armageddon' outta here!"—Ed Strnad

The Millennium approaches. Humankind hangs on tenterhooks anticipating this Great Event. A time to marvel; a time to speculate. A new age; or an apocalypse.

We the editors of *The Optimist's/Pessimist's Guide to the Millennium* designed this book to be an irreverent peek into the unseen future. This task called for a unique approach. To bring you both the "good news" and the "bad news" about the shape of things to come, we sought the most divergent, polar-opposite points of view possible.

Barbara Ann Kipfer is author of the irrepressibly cheery *14,000 things to be happy about, 14,000 things for kids to be happy about*, and Page-a-Day calendars. She sees the proverbial water glass as half full. Ed Strnad is author of the incorrigibly irascible *1401 Things That P*ss Me Off* trilogy. To him, the glass is shattered; people are cutting themselves. Kipfer and Strnad are thus the perfect pair to paint portraits of that two-faced Janus called "The Millennium."

We commissioned these two to peer into their respective bright and dark crystal balls, to compare and contrast their whimsical/hellish visions, and to report their prescient forecasts in a concise, "she said/he said" format. But we worried. Would bringing together our Pollyanna prophetess with our crotchety Cassandra result in an explosion, like matter touching antimatter? Only time will tell; as editors, we prefer to take a balanced stance and leave the predictions for others to mull over.

One thing we are sure of is that Kipfer and Strnad's effort is nothing short of amazing. And unlike that gloomy-Gus prognosticator, Nostradamus, the 21st century that Barbara and Ed envision will be fantastic and funny! We think you'll wholeheartedly agree.

Looking for a map of the high and low spots on the Road to Tomorrow? Forearm yourself with the foresights in *The Optimist's/Pessimist's Guide to the Millennium*, and prepare to boldly go where no one has gone before—into the future. Regardless of whether you're an optimist or a pessimist, the next millennium is where you'll spend the rest of your life. You might as well meet it with a smile—or at least a slight smirk.

😋 "Have a nice Millennium!" —B.A.K.

😒 "Wake me when it's over." —E.S.

☽ the new adventures of the 21st century
> **☀ there will be unimaginable horrors and cataclysms, and we won't live to see most of them**

◎

☽ TVs that turn off when nobody is listening or watching
> **☀ TVs and radios that the government can turn on whenever it wants**

◎

☽ "dictating" your work to a computer that spells everything correctly
> **☀ memos from your dictation machine full of "uhhs," "ummms," and "This should satisfy that twerp boss of mine"**

◎

☽ cars that can do warp speed
> **☀ average freeway speed will be 12 mph**

1

The Optimist's /Pessimist's Guide to the Millennium

☻ calculators and computers for every student
☹ kids who can't add or spell without their PC

◎

☻ diaries that turn into secret code when opened by intruders
☹ books that self-immolate after one reading to prevent illegal copying

◎

☻ the return of forgiveness and tolerance
☹ the return of the Captain and Tenille

◎

☻ everyone will be allowed to vote—it will be a given right
☹ President Quayle

◎

☻ good, honest government officials
☹ four more words you won't be able to say without laughing: Vice-President Sonny Bono

☙ starting over economically: 1-cent candy, 5-cent phone calls, salaries lowered, goods and services lowered accordingly...

> **☙ zillions of old coots reminiscing about the '60s**

◎

☙ drug-free workplaces

> **☙ workplace toilets that will surreptitiously test for drugs**

◎

☙ a ban on yelling on TV or radio shows

> **☙ a "SMILE" control on TVs and radios for people who want happy news**

◎

☙ a new happy attitude from sea to shining sea

> **☙ Prozac will be added to the water supply of New York and Los Angeles**

◎

☙ the exciting prospect of interplanetary travel

> **☙ on a 35-million-mile trip to Mars, the number of times your kids will ask, "Are we there YET?"**

3

🌢 communication with other planets
> **🐾 calling a wrong planet on your "communicator"**

◎

🌢 a sensor that stops your car the correct distance behind another car or obstruction
> **🐾 evolution will eventually cause all motorists' unused left legs to shrivel up**

◎

🌢 mini-size makeup and toiletries for travel
> **🐾 "car commode" built into seats— still not perfected**

◎

🌢 a plethora of older parents who waited for wisdom and maturity to arrive before their children did
> **🐾 a "rent-a-dad" service to play with kids whose dads are too old for rugged sports and other strenuous activities**

◎

🌢 a machine that cleans shoes before you enter the house
> **🐾 a "mommy robot"**

☻ appliances that indicate what part is broken

> ☹ **talking appliances that say "Kiss your money good-bye" when they break**

◎

☻ a fat-dissolving pill to take after a sinful meal

> ☹ **fat-dissolving pill will have one little side effect— the munchies**

◎

☻ cleanliness laws enforced and upheld in public places and on public transportation

> ☹ **you will need a token and a tetanus shot before entering the subway**

◎

☻ anti-graffiti coating for buildings

> ☹ **sky-written graffiti, thanks to vandals wearing new-fangled rocket packs**

◎

☻ a law requiring everyone to vote

> ☹ **people will be too apathetic to vote for a mandatory-voting law**

5

☻ an end to poor workmanship

☹ "Made in USA" will become a warning label

◎

☻ political commercials replaced by a kinder, more informative presentation of the candidates

☹ a 24-hour Nasty Channel on cable that runs nothing but negative campaign ads

◎

☻ fresh candy and popcorn at theaters

☹ the giant-size tub of movie popcorn must be purchased with a life insurance policy

◎

☻ uplifting movies that don't cater to the lowest common denominator

☹ *Rocky XIII* and *Terminator-5* will still be big box office attractions

◎

☻ a product that gives you hair where you need or want it

☹ the fear of random violence will be replaced by the fear of going bald

6

☻ the "spirit of Christmas" all year long
> ☹ **retailers will establish a second, "mid-year," Christmas on June 25th**

◎

☻ TV shows that improve teenage literacy
> ☹ **Beavis and Butt-head will host** *Masterpiece Theater*

◎

☻ no more Elvis sightings
> ☹ **Elvis will crash-land a UFO into Loch Ness, killing "Nessy"**

◎

☻ safe sparklers, firecrackers, and other fireworks
> ☹ **"safe" guns with "less harmful" bullets will be promoted by the NRA**

◎

☻ twenty-twenty vision for all
> ☹ **optometrist jokes will run riot in the year 2020**

☽ pens that don't leak or blob

☾ pens and pencils will become quaint curiosities

◎

☽ an easy, foolproof way to clean pet teeth

☾ dentures for pets

◎

☽ a required art course every year in every school

☾ computer graphics will replace fingerpainting in classrooms

◎

☽ human space migration and colonization burgeon

☾ Martians will say, "Well, there goes the solar system"

◎

☽ new leaders will boldly guide the country into the unseen future

☾ the world will be run by Generation X-ers

◎

☽ we finally switch to the metric system

☾ we finally switch to the metric system

☽ the average life expectancy climbs to 100–110
  ☽ **the average IQ declines to 90–100**

◎

☽ a woman president
  ☽ **a female pope (yeah, right)**

◎

☽ *14,000 things to be happy about* by Barbara Ann Kipfer sells over a million copies
  ☽ **1401 Things That P*ss Me Off by Ed Strnad is made into a zany movie starring Bruce Willis**

◎

☽ having a bright new age to rejoice in
  ☽ **having to get all your checks reprinted with "20__" in the date**

◎

☽ the closing moment of 1999
  ☽ **the "Countdown to Christ"**

☽ hearty greetings and salutations for the new age

☟ **corny coworkers—who usually say "See you next year" every December 31st—will get to quip "See you next MILLENNIUM!"**

◉

☽ deep introspection over what humankind has wrought over the last millennium

☟ **endless "Best and Worst of the Millennium" lists by every critic**

◉

☽ an invention that replaces photograph negatives with something you can see

☟ **you'll discover that photos of you are much more flattering when Vaseline is smeared on the lens**

◉

☽ garbage that disintegrates once crumpled

☟ **garbage will get recycled into new TV shows**

◉

☽ animal adoption programs

☟ **owning any living creature will be politically incorrect**

☽ commercials when you want them, but otherwise—none
> ☌ **ubiquitous ads in restroom stalls, checkout lines, while on hold, etc.**

◎

☽ the information superhighway becomes operational
> ☌ **the 500-channel information superhighway will consist of 300 home-shopping channels, 60 channels of country-western line dancing, and an *OJ: The Post-Trial Years* channel**

◎

☽ a TV guide for the discriminating viewer listing only informative shows
> ☌ **with 500 channels, TV guides will be the size of phone books**

◎

☽ we will reap the fruits of advanced technology
> ☌ **two identical snowflakes will be found**

11

😊 eyeglasses that don't break
> 😦 millions to suffer permanently blurred vision from having gazed at "Magic-Eye" 3-D books in the '90s

◎

😊 cellular phones with perfect signals all the time
> 😦 you'll have to don a lead helmet to use a cellular phone and stay tumor-free

◎

😊 discovery of life on another planet
> 😦 first visitor from another planet will be deported as an illegal alien

◎

😊 lightning-fast PCs
> 😦 faster computers will enable you to be wrong much more quickly

◎

😊 music by the next generation of superstars
> 😦 we will have the music of Michael "Elvis Jr." Jackson to look forward to

☻ everyone will be famous for fifteen minutes

> ☻ getting your moment in the sun will be tough once the ozone layer disappears

◎

☻ international telephone communications without the delay

> ☻ "21st Century Fox" just won't have the same ring to it

◎

☻ college for everyone, no matter what their finances

> ☻ thanks to lowered educational standards, everyone will get straight A's

◎

☻ a safe cure for obesity

> ☻ willpower won't come in a pill

◎

☻ women will not have to wear dresses to work

> ☻ men will still have to wear ties

- once-commonplace items will become collectibles
  - **your collection of comic books would be worth jillions, had your mother not thrown them out**

- a smoke-free world
  - **the rise of extremist "Smokers' Rights" groups**

- dents that pop back out on cars
  - **you will drive a great big air bag on wheels**

- getting to enjoy the nest egg you built over the years
  - **the money you saved for a rainy day won't get you through a heavy dew**

- children's playtime will no longer involve TV or VCRs
  - **TV/VCR controls will be built into furniture so couch potatoes won't have to expend energy reaching for the remote**

☻ schools run by successful businesses or professional
business people

☹ McDonald's Hamburger University will become
an institute of higher learning

◎

☻ the return of air you can't see

☹ smog levels equivalent to inhaling iron filings

◎

☻ the world wired for communication

☹ freak electrical storms will temporarily cripple
phones, faxes, and modems, forcing people to
actually speak to each other face to face

◎

☻ safe child care

☹ kids who were put in child care will
later warehouse their elderly parents in
"Senior Care" facilities

15

☺ VCRs as simple to use as radios and TVs
> ☹ **billions of VCRs will still be flashing
> "12:00 . . . 12:00 . . . 12:00 . . ."**

◎

☺ immigration to overcrowded areas will be outlawed
> ☹ **"The Great Wall of Xenophobia" to be built along
> US-Mexico border**

◎

☺ affordable health care and insurance for all
> ☹ **health-care decisions will become drastically
> simpler, thanks to pre-admission wallet X rays**

◎

☺ breaking the time barrier
> ☹ **time travel will be possible, but for technical
> reasons you can only visit the 1970s**

◎

☺ cryogenics is available
> ☹ **cryogenics' major downside will be nasty
> freezer burn**

16

☯ people will be thinner, more active, less frantic, more secure, and healthier

> **☯ the market for cosmetic surgery and health fads will explode**

◎

☯ oldsters will cherish memories of youthful abandon and wild living

> **☯ a good night of sleep will be preferable to a good night of sex**

◎

☯ game shows eliminated from broadcast television

> **☯ unemployed game-show hosts will swell the welfare rolls**

◎

☯ nuclear power plants become extinct

> **☯ many things become extinct: frogs, turtles, civility, Democrats**

◎

☯ wrist telephones

> **☯ wrist-phones always ring when you're in the tub**

17

☙ gas engines will be compact and more efficient
  ☙ gasoline will be five dollars a gallon

◉

☙ surrendering gracefully to the years
  ☙ oldsters pushing AM/FM stereo-equipped
    walkers

◉

☙ Disneyland will become the 51st state
  ☙ Goofy will be elected the first governor

◉

☙ control of immigration
  ☙ migrant labor pools will dry up and car wash,
    gardening, child care, and restaurant industries
    will collapse

◉

☙ the decommercialization of Christmas
  ☙ kids will e-mail Santa @*northpole.com*

☻ a product that replaces flossing
> ☹ toothless, "gummy" look will come into vogue

◎

☻ cheap transportation for all
> ☹ if cost and size trends continue, a 2010 Toyota will cost a million dollars and fit on the head of a pin

◎

☻ a PC in every hotel room
> ☹ Dr. Kevorkian will start a chain of euthanasia motels with guaranteed fast "check-out"

◎

☻ new forms of music to appreciate
> ☹ all new music will sound too damn loud, and the words will be unintelligible

19

😋 magazines on CD-ROM

> 🐍 **CD-ROM version of *Playboy* will fizzle, as computers prove too awkward to hold sideways with one hand**

◎

😋 old movies will be un-colorized

> 🐍 **"audio-ization" process will allow Hollywood to dub sound onto old silent films**

◎

😋 inter-species communication established

> 🐍 **it will be possible for your cat to kvetch about her food**

◎

😋 floating cities in oceans will help spread out the population

> 🐍 **first floating city to be named "Dramamine-Land"**

◎

😋 being able to gain or lose weight in a healthy, foolproof way

> 🐍 **you won't be able to eat *anything* without a twinge of guilt**

☾ computers will be able to interpret complex patterns of data
>**☞ it will be a chore to decipher the old tattoos on someone's wrinkled hide**

◎

☾ cheap energy created through fusion
>**☞ oil companies still suppressing car engines that can run on water**

◎

☾ first human clone
>**☞ robotic version of Henry Kissinger will be indistinguishable from the original**

◎

☾ cheap designer clothing
>**☞ everyone will be dressed like the Jetsons**

◎

☾ retirement before 65 with full pension
>**☞ retirement age will be raised to 75**

◎

☾ being allowed to sit and read in any bookstore
>**☞ espresso shops will take over bookstores**

😃 a honeymoon on the moon is possible
> **😈 restaurants on the moon won't have any "atmosphere"**

◎

😃 the *Titanic* becomes a museum
> **😈 there will be disaster-motif hotels: The Sheraton Titanic, The Marriott at 3 Mile Island, The Hindenburg Inn, The Black Hole of Calcutta Chateau**

◎

😃 "unsinkable" swimsuits for children
> **😈 electronic tethers for errant children**

◎

😃 cloth will be totally resistant to dirt and stains
> **😈 the soup-repellent tie will still be in the lab**

◎

😃 newspapers that don't get your hands dirty
> **😈 all newspapers will be electronic—reading one in the tub will get you electrocuted**

☽ computers that can automatically and accurately translate foreign language texts

> ☝ computers still can't decipher the words to "Louie, Louie"

◎

☽ shoulder pads go out of style

> ☝ everyone will take to wearing a fez

◎

☽ a cure for PMS

> ☝ a hat with a retracting ray-gun will sell briskly

◎

☽ "New and Improved" products must pass a test to prove they are

> ☝ "Space Age" products will seem awfully dated

◎

☽ generation gaps will close

> ☝ there will be an abundance of grandmothers named Grandma Bambi (Stacy, Candy, Caitlin, etc.)

🌳 a 2000 "Millennium Edition" of the VW Beetle
　　🌿 **lots of other callow products will try to make a buck off the millennium**

◎

🌳 an effective way to dissuade kids from using drugs
　　🌿 **Hard Rock Cafes will put rock stars' drug-ravaged livers on display**

◎

🌳 an emphasis on personal accountability will reign
　　🌿 **the Statue of Liberty will be knocked off her pedestal by the new Statue of Responsibility**

◎

🌳 harmony and understanding abound
　　🌿 **endless bickering over whether 2001 should be pronounced "Two-thousand-and-one" or "Twenty-oh-one"**

◎

🌳 hopeful millions looking forward to the beginning of a bright New Age
　　🌿 **doomsday "Zero Zeitgeisters" predicting millennial Armageddon**

☻ simplified telephone systems so you don't have to fumble around for numbers, buttons, or special codes

> **☹ in 9 out of 10 phone calls, you will not reach a live human being**

◎

☻ cleanup of the world's dumping grounds

> **☹ to appear environmentally friendly, toxic waste will be packed in recyclable containers**

◎

☻ drive-thru delis

> **☹ drive-thru liquor stores**

◎

☻ jobs not yet invented will come into being

> **☹ there will be lots of work for "Safety-Net Dismantlers" in the Republican party**

◎

☻ passenger flights on the space shuttle

> **☹ zero-gravity restrooms**

25

☺ no more change of life

☹ **menopausal boomers who can't distinguish between hot flashes and acid flashbacks**

◎

☺ figuring out a system so no one is lonely in this world of billions of people

☹ **everyone will be assigned a lifelong "buddy" at birth**

◎

☺ a way discovered to make men and women get along better without having to read how-to books

☹ **men will move to Mars, women to Venus**

◎

☺ a thousand years of peace and tranquility

☹ **the entire planet will wet its collective pants every few years from near collisions with giant asteroids**

26

desserts with no calories and no chemicals
> **chocolate will be declared an addictive substance; Senate investigators will grill Hershey executives**

◎

100% successful cataract surgeries
> **Little Orphan Annie will finally be given pupil transplants**

◎

all automobiles will have electronic collision-avoidance hardware
> **all cars will be bulletproof**

◎

the secrets of Atlantis found
> **Donald Trump will raise Atlantis and turn it into Atlantis City Hotel and Casino**

◎

one good local newspaper per town
> **New York Post's last headline will be: "World Ends; We Win"**

☽ the removal of all incompetent drivers by revoking their licenses

> ☽ **stiff prison sentences for breaking the speed of light**

◎

☽ really permanent hair color

> ☽ **gray and white hair never become trendy**

◎

☽ happy therapy replacing psychotherapy

> ☽ **therapists will help you recover memories of past enjoyment**

◎

☽ the emergence of self-confident, self-sufficient, tolerant, good-natured people

> ☽ **the spectacle of hyperactive, frenetic people near the end trying to make up for an unremarkable life**

◎

☽ a novel way to control population will be found

> ☽ **more people will be abducted by aliens than ever before**

28

☺ dollar bills that stay clean and don't wrinkle
> ☹ **the Susan B. Anthony dollar will be trotted out again**

◎

☺ computers with voice-recognition technology
> ☹ **wiseguys blurting out "Erase hard disk" to your voice-controlled, but not voice-recognizing, PC**

◎

☺ TV replaced by reading as the main form of entertainment
> ☹ **TV will be replaced by virtual reality, especially the "feely" type**

◎

☺ TRIX cereal for adults
> ☹ ***Playboy Jr.* magazine for kids**

◎

☺ laser surgery replaces tonsillectomies
> ☹ **doctors will discover that you *need* your tonsils, after all**

29

☻ underwater cities are built
☹ Atlantic-Americans won't get along too swimmingly with Pacific-Americans

◎

☻ people living longer and healthier lives
☹ aging athletes will look like beef jerky in Nikes

◎

☻ an overall feeling of respect for others' traditions and cultures
☹ giggling at others will be outlawed

◎

☻ garbage trucks that separate trash for recycling
☹ by sorting trash you'll unwittingly become an unpaid employee of your local trash-collection company

◎

☻ no more religious misunderstandings
☹ Maury Povich will be revealed as the anti-Christ

◎

☻ bees that don't sting
☹ killer bees will invade all 48 contiguous states

🌙 slavery abolished in all countries
> 🐍 electronic ID badges will let the boss keep tabs on you at work

◎

🌙 civilization will advance
> 🐍 new wars will kill you in new ways

◎

🌙 classic rock songs will be rediscovered
> 🐍 remakes of songs for older rockers,
> e.g.: "Hey, You, Get Offa My Lawn . . .";
> "Born to Be Wild—Within Reason . . ."

◎

🌙 prenatal care for all
> 🐍 ultrasounds will be in color with
> Dolby-stereo sound

◎

🌙 pants that never lose their pleats
> 🐍 no clothing (shirts, etc.) will ever be tucked
> in anymore

31

☻ heated roads and driveways that melt snow and ice
　　☹ **all urban roads in permanent gridlock**

◎

☻ four weeks' vacation a year
　　☹ **the 30-hour workweek will be just another
　　unfulfilled promise of the future**

◎

☻ no fee on all credit cards
　　☹ **most places won't take cash anymore**

◎

☻ easy-to-remove hermetic seals and shrink wrap
　　☹ **packaging will be so tamperproof even the buyer
　　won't be able to open it**

◎

☻ mandatory courses for using libraries and reference books
　　☹ **all library books will be on compact laser discs
　　that no one will know how to operate**

☺ a device that detects carjackers
> ☹ instead of a siren that people ignore,
> your car's alarm will scream out your name
> while being stolen

◎

☺ someone will run a 3-minute mile
> ☹ faster-acting laxatives

◎

☺ safe schools
> ☹ the return of paddling to the school system

◎

☺ a dramatic lowering of the divorce rate
> ☹ legions of people with those hyphenated
> last names

◎

☺ "smart" ovens
> ☹ most people still won't know how their toaster
> knows when the bread is done

33

😋 skim milk that looks and tastes like whole

> 😾 **too many milk-product choices: "whey-out" style, from free-range cows, I Can't Believe It's Not Lactose!, etc.**

◎

😋 a qualifying test for babysitters

> 😾 **prospective employers will analyze a sample of babysitter's hair for drugs, alcohol, etc.**

◎

😋 more creativity classes for children

> 😾 **active, creative kids will be given drugs to behave more "normally"**

◎

😋 the opportunity for all to work

> 😾 **all the kids your mom wouldn't let you play with will be in positions of authority**

◎

😋 a choice of pillow hardness at hotels

> 😾 **there will be 3,000 salad dressings to choose from at salad bars**

34

☻ silent appliances
> ☹ louder will still mean "better"—in tools, talk, and bombs

◎

☻ background music in every room of your house
> ☹ Muzak will make music videos that are shown in elevators and supermarkets

◎

☻ only healthy junk food
> ☹ whole-grain Pop-Tarts

◎

☻ fewer factories with visible smokestacks
> ☹ more factories that emit invisible radiation

◎

☻ an innovative replacement for landfills
> ☹ archaeologists unearth the first fossilized disposable diaper

35

😃 seagulls that stay by the seashore

> 😾 **birds equipped with laser-targeting excretion technology**

◎

😃 the end of Styrofoam

> 😾 **everything will come packed in stale popcorn**

◎

😃 a fuel that becomes fresh air before it is discharged into the atmosphere

> 😾 **air that you can see and *taste***

◎

😃 cities free of crime

> 😾 **police armed with automatic weapons on every street corner**

◎

😃 people living without the fear of death

> 😾 **the fear of death will lose its wonderful power to motivate**

☻ more three-day weekends

> ☹ you won't be able to use "death of a grandparent" as an excuse for a day off from work anymore

◎

☻ people exercising for fun

> ☹ the favorite exercise of the future—jogging your memories

◎

☻ VCRs that program themselves

> ☹ virtual reality devices will be programmed with Steven Spielberg's nightmares

◎

☻ outlets that cannot electrocute someone

> ☹ new electrical cords with four prongs won't plug into your three-hole outlets

◎

☻ the existence of UFOs is officially announced

> ☹ the source of UFOs will be traced to Cleveland

☻ the ability to predict earthquakes
> ☹ wild panics will ensue after the warning, "EARTHQUAKE IN 10 MINUTES!"

◎

☻ anyone who can work from home is allowed to
> ☹ millions of at-home workers will never get a chance to shoot rubber bands at coworkers

◎

☻ videophonic intercommunication for all
> ☹ you'll see as well as hear the obnoxious invaders of your privacy

◎

☻ TV will be 3-dimensional holographs
> ☹ we'll watch wide-screen, 3-D holographic reruns of *The Brady Bunch*

◎

☻ a cure for the common cold is found
> ☹ it will be acknowledged that the cure for colds was in chicken soup all along

☻ astronomers discover the origin of the solar system
☹ our universe will turn out to be just a dust bunny under a giant's bed

◎

☻ cat litter that disintegrates the waste and is odorless
☹ android pets that leave synthetic droppings on your Astroturf lawn

◎

☻ a waning interest in the media and a new respect for privacy
☹ the invasiveness of computers will make privacy rarer than rocking-horse manure

◎

☻ a ban on cutting down trees
☹ no more real Christmas trees

◎

☻ pizza at the movies
☹ "pepperoni-flavored" topping for your movie pizza will cost extra

39

☻ safe X rays

> ☹ **people who have been getting regular X rays since childhood begin to glow softly in the dark**

◎

☻ elevators that tell jokes since everyone is so serious in them

> ☹ **practical joker elevators that close their doors faster when they sense you running toward them**

◎

☻ a cure for mall headache

> ☹ **retro-malls will be designed to look like '50s drugstores**

◎

☻ computers will file all our taxes automatically

> ☹ **thanks to our friend the computer, the IRS will be able to audit 9 out of 10 returns**

◎

☻ bathing suits that stay in place

> ☹ **ego-enhancing inflatable swim trunks for men**

40

☻ graduating in 2000
> ☹ a college education will cost $2,000—a week

◎

☻ static-free clothing
> ☹ you'll get lots of static if you wear your old Nehru jacket again

◎

☻ easy-to-follow instructions for everything
> ☹ unfortunately, the future will not come with operating instructions

◎

☻ paid sick days in every job
> ☹ future medical insurance programs will consist of just three words: Don't get sick

◎

☻ a device that locates empty parking spaces at shopping malls
> ☹ a ticket will be issued for even *thinking* of parking on some New York City streets

41

☺ an end to the stigmatization of therapy
>   ☹ **therapy's going rate will be over $300 per hour, or $5,000 per personality quirk**

◎

☺ a machine that changes the color of clothes so you only have to buy one color of a style
>   ☹ **leisure suits that change color from white to lime-green throughout the day**

◎

☺ bays and coastlines will be cleaned up
>   ☹ **whatever seafood is still nontoxic will be totally unaffordable**

◎

☺ people laughing *with* others, not *at* them
>   ☹ **shortages of silliness**

◎

☺ inexpensive immunization for pets
>   ☹ **pets will receive better health care than most humans**

☽ a national newspaper of only good news and success stories
☾ there will be no reminders in the media that there are people smarter than you

◎

☽ all regular ties will be replaced by clip-ons
☾ "power ties" will actually radiate repulsive force fields

◎

☽ high school education required for every job
☾ graduate degrees required to flip burgers

◎

☽ fewer, better brands to choose from in the grocery store
☾ Heinz's 3,457 varieties

◎

☽ pollution-free automobiles
☾ smog-belching buses will continue to be exempt from emission-control laws

😋 no more world wars

🅿 everyone will just *sue* everyone else instead of waging war

◎

😋 no more midlife crisis

🅿 your inner child will hit middle age

◎

😋 life skills will be taught in high school and college

🅿 neo-yuppie kids will go from *Sesame Street* to *Wall Street Week in Review*

◎

😋 there will be low-fat versions of all snacks

🅿 diet Slim Jims and no-fat Twinkies

◎

😋 school buses with seat belts

🅿 buses will be known as "loser-cruisers"

◎

😋 porta-potties for pets

🅿 doggie day care centers

😊 the world does *not* come to an end in 2000
    😠 ditto

◎

😊 fast-food chains go upscale
    😠 Rack of Lamb On-a-Stick; McChateaubriand; Jacques-in-le-Box

◎

😊 the end of fabrics that wrinkle
    😠 the dawning of the Age of Spandex

◎

😊 services that offer on-line demonstrations of recipes
    😠 on-line confession for computer-savvy Catholics

◎

😊 a test given to candidates to qualify them to run for office
    😠 virtual 3-D hologram politicians will make "live" speeches in your living room

◎

😊 a cure for insomnia
    😠 a 24-hour golf channel

45

☺ revival of the "block party"
     ☹ numerous yard sales of used lava lamps

◎

☺ genetically-altered onions will make you laugh
     ☹ gene-splicing will produce cats with wings

◎

☺ teaching manners in grade school
     ☹ third graders "packing iron"

◎

☺ abolition of all nuclear weapons
     ☹ the ultimate weapon will be a bomb that turns everyone the same color

◎

☺ technologies are used appropriately
     ☹ scientists will use the Hubbell telescope to watch people undressing on Earth

◎

☺ computers will prescribe medication
     ☹ "Take two aspirins and boot me up in the morning"

☻ transcontinental travel time reduced to one hour
> **☹ it will take less and less time to get to Europe, and more and more time to get to work**

◎

☻ cars will float on cushions of air
> **☹ in your dotage you'll drive enormous old cars big enough to land jet aircraft on**

◎

☻ vitamin therapy by injection
> **☹ old druggies mainlining Geritol**

◎

☻ driverless automobiles
> **☹ brainless drivers**

◎

☻ areas of Texas and California are split to form new states
> **☹ "Texmex" and "Frisco" admitted to the Union in 2001**

😊 clean beaches
> 😠 you'll have to wipe your feet when you come out of the ocean

◎

😊 nail polish that doesn't chip
> 😠 nail polish for men will be introduced (in "Macho Black & Blue" colors)

◎

😊 shoes that conform to your foot shape
> 😠 you'll worry more about how your shoes fit than how your sweater does

◎

😊 no need for antennas on anything
> 😠 obsolete satellite-TV dishes will become big expensive birdbaths

◎

😊 a way to script your dreams
> 😠 revivals of TV shows that were rancid the first time around will give you nightmares

48

☉ a way discovered to fix a broken heart
☉ the FDA won't approve Time-in-a-Bottle as cardiac-repair medicine

◎

☉ ignorance is no longer accepted as an excuse
☉ ignorance still won't be painful

◎

☉ grunge music goes out of style
☉ rap-chanting monks will be all the rage

◎

☉ exercise gain with no pain
☉ pushing 50 will be enough exercise for most people

◎

☉ drive-thru post offices
☉ postal employees will give you a 10-second head start before they start shooting

😋 a cure for baldness
> 🙀 **Greek men become follicle donors for hair transplants**

◎

😋 a cure for argumentativeness
> 🙀 **the return of gun duels to settle disputes**

◎

😋 austerity is in
> 🙀 **everyone will be p*ssed at the poor**

◎

😋 autumn colors can be preserved longer
> 🙀 **the yellow traffic signal will officially mean "floor it"**

◎

😋 a realization by many people that they should live simpler lives
> 🙀 **a million bucks won't buy what it used to**

◎

😋 more soap operas at night
> 🙀 **daytime TV will be solid talk shows**

☙ the government stops spending more on prisons than
on education
> **☙ telethons to raise money to build prisons**

◎

☙ TV becomes more entertaining and less violent
> **☙ Fox network wins rights to televise executions**

◎

☙ *Sesame Street* still on TV
> **☙ *Sesame Street* will *not* be brought to you by the
> letters G, O, and P**

◎

☙ making your resolution for 2000 in 1999
> **☙ breaking your resolution for 2000 in 1999**

◎

☙ people think very differently (*more optimistic!*) in 2000
> **☙ people think pretty much the same (*pessimistically*)
> in 2000**

☻ painless dentistry

    ☹ your teeth will still be pulled by automatons who tell bad jokes

◎

☻ accurate news/facts required from the media

    ☹ the *Enquirer* will be more believable than TV news

◎

☻ a new order of peace

    ☹ the "Star Wars" program will be revived

◎

☻ no more waiting rooms in doctors' offices

    ☹ most of the numbers in your "little black book" will belong to doctors

◎

☻ curtains that adjust to let light through or block it

    ☹ it will be too smoggy to see rainbows in color, only in shades of gray

52

☻ housing for the homeless
　　☹ (tax) shelters for the rich

◎

☻ advance-to-the-next-song control on all tape players
　　☹ you'll find yourself switching from classic-rock radio stations to easy-listening stations

◎

☻ incentives for jury duty to make it tolerable
　　☹ all crimes will be tried by the media

◎

☻ less military involvement overseas
　　☹ the United States still playing "Globocop"

◎

☻ a ban on weapons and the destruction of those that exist
　　☹ watch for new weapons of nondestruction, like the Super-Glue Bomb

◎

☻ a safe form of birth control
　　☹ warning labels will be printed on your body parts (e.g., "Do Not Touch!")

53

☻ rock 'n' roll turns 50
　　　☹ **the Rolling Stones turn 60**

◎

☻ bookstores replacing bars as the place to meet
　　　☹ **blood-testing clinics become the new hot spot for first dates**

◎

☻ the return of home cooking
　　　☹ **restaurants that serve nothing but Spam dishes (Spam-O-Ramas)**

◎

☻ electronic mail replaces first-class mail
　　　☹ **it will cost 50 cents to mail a letter, assuming anyone still knows how to write**

◎

☻ good-tasting microwave pizza
　　　☹ **we'll be able to put a man on Mars, but *still* won't be able to put metal in a microwave**

54

Monday Night Football starts an hour earlier
> **cities will be destroyed by football fans whenever their team wins the Super Bowl**

◎

baseball gets new rules to speed it up and make it more interesting
> **baseball will be made into a contact sport, featuring "clubbing," "short-stopping," and "3 strikes and you're unconscious"**

◎

crash proof computers
> **PC data vandal-hackers will form a new criminal class**

◎

crash proof helicopters
> **newspapers won't get to report a helicopter accident and use the word "decapitated"**

◎

a cure for alcoholism
> **a "sober-up" drug**

☻ a return to the original formula for Dairy Queen ice cream
> ☹ you will say "things were better in the good old days," and be right

◉

☻ cars that get 100 miles to the gallon
> ☹ your Time Machine will only get five years to the gallon

◉

☻ a chance to return to a previous point in your life—and change it
> ☹ no "Undo" button for your life

◉

☻ a friendly, understanding IRS
> ☹ your paychecks will be issued directly from the IRS (after "appropriate" deductions, of course)

◉

☻ being able to get your picture on a postage stamp
> ☹ people will spit on both sides of the new Nixon stamp

56

☺ DNA research will eliminate most congenital diseases

> ☹ there'll be incredible medical miracles, like a doctor showing up for an appointment on time

◎

☺ the end of infomercials

> ☹ a 24-hour Ginsu knife channel

◎

☺ America is governed by electronic democratic consensus rather than politicians

> ☹ Russia is still driving toward democracy, but will run over a few republics along the way

◎

☺ the Social Security system will be healthy

> ☹ Social Security will go belly-up by the time you're eligible for it

57

☽ no more trashy talk shows

> ☆ there will be an obsession with the "normal," as opposed to the dysfunctional

◎

☽ a higher appreciation for arts and culture

> ☆ Los Angeles will be the center of the arts and tractor pulls will be the major cultural event

◎

☽ books that never flip closed and lose your place

> ☆ books will be given ratings like movies, i.e., *G, PG, R, NC-17*

◎

☽ a crystal ball that tells the truth

> ☆ erstwhile psychics will form "Prediction Companies" that cater to the pathetic human need for certainty

◎

☽ calendar pages that change automatically

> ☆ each decade will seem to pass twice as fast as the previous decade

58

☻ space satellites give us all we ever wanted to know about space
> ☹ **ultrasophisticated communications satellites will be used to bring us reruns of *Ren & Stimpy***

◎

☻ space tourism is a big success
> ☹ **rocket-lag turns out to be a hundred times worse than jet-lag**

◎

☻ long-range, accurate weather forecasts become possible
> ☹ **forgetting your umbrella remains the most surefire way to make it rain**

◎

☻ ethics taught in all schools
> ☹ **business ethics books will be found in the library's "fiction" section**

◎

☻ home computers schedule our work and anticipate our every need
> ☹ **human dependency on computers will cause our brains to atrophy**

59

☙ freedom from dependence on lawyers
> ☙ at current rates, by the year 2075 every man, woman, and child will be a lawyer

◎

☙ the JFK assassination controversy will finally be settled
> ☙ new conspiracy theory will claim Elvis shot Kennedy

◎

☙ we find out the identity of Watergate's Deep Throat
> ☙ (it was Nixon's non-evil twin brother)

◎

☙ new species of plants and animals are cultured
> ☙ city pigeons mutate into something resembling a molting Goodyear blimp

◎

☙ waste recycling is a major industry
> ☙ someone will write a best-seller, *101 Uses for Used Dental Floss*

◎

☙ a cure for stiff necks and aching backs
> ☙ planetariums will be shut down

☻ nice guys finishing first
☹ **pessimists burning their bridges ahead of them**

◎

☻ resolving droughts with creative means
☹ **the invention of instant water**

◎

☻ preventing forest fires
☹ **due to dwindling forest acreage, Smoky the Bear will campaign for Urban Gentrification Programs**

◎

☻ computers creating jobs, not doing away with them
☹ **workers will be replaced by computers that can grovel**

◎

☻ Kid's Day joining Mother's Day and Father's Day
☹ **greeting card companies will invent new bogus holidays to sell more cards: Proud to Be Me Day, Brunette Day, Five Foot and Over Day, etc.**

☻ no more parking meters

☹ meters that impound your car with tractor beams until the amount due is paid

◎

☻ wishing wells with guarantees

☹ lawsuits lodged against wells that don't grant wishes

◎

☻ very high taxes eliminate alcohol as a commodity

☹ rich alcoholics will obtain black-market livers for their transplant operations

◎

☻ Rush Limbaugh retires

☹ Rush Limbaugh will have the heart of a liberal—in a jar on his desk

◎

☻ everything made to last 10 times longer

☹ the rush hour will last from 12 noon to 10 P.M.

62

❧ repossessed vacant buildings used by cities for community
centers, day care, or housing

> **Sears Tower will be converted into the World's
> Tallest Bungee Jump**

◎

❧ intelligent life found in space

> **the search for intelligent life on Earth goes on**

◎

❧ glue that really works

> **no glue invented to fix broken homes**

◎

❧ methods developed to raise IQs

> **new "Smarty Pants" will increase your IQ *and*
> make a fashion statement**

◎

❧ computers simple enough to be operated by a four-year-old

> **you'll have to locate a four-year-old to make your
> PC work**

63

🖐 automatic computer programming replaces much human programming of computers

> 🐾 **your most frequently used computer language will be "@!#?!%&!*!"**

◎

🖐 large screen video walls change your environment or art

> 🐾 **wide-screen TVs will make it possible to watch Jay Leno's chins multiply over the years**

◎

🖐 flat screen TVs

> 🐾 **wall-hanging TV screens will always be "just 10 years away"**

◎

🖐 alternatives to animal testing found

> 🐾 **the Three Blind Mice to have vision-restoration surgery**

◎

🖐 a way found to delay memory loss

> 🐾 **it will take until 2030 to forget the Reagan years**

😋 fresh new musical styles

😋 comeback tours by '80s bands

◎

😋 artificial Christmas trees that don't lose needles

😋 Christmas trees that morph into a menorah at the touch of a button

◎

😋 a cure for video-game addiction

😋 longtime game players will get thumb transplants

◎

😋 space-age foods

😋 taste-tempting meals-in-a-pill washed down with Tang

◎

😋 soft butter or margarine in restaurants

😋 butter will top a list of outlawed unhealthy products

☺ electric cars become practical
>☹ nasty sticker shock when buying an electric car

◎

☺ grand tours of the solar system
>☹ space tourists will still wear flowered shirts and Bermuda shorts

◎

☺ the end of televangelism
>☹ mail-order religions will spring up

◎

☺ elimination of harmful chemicals and radiation from the environment
>☹ Calvin Klein to market lead underwear to counteract the declining rate of male potency

◎

☺ the enormous potential of virtual reality
>☹ the enormous potential of VR to exacerbate loneliness

☽ elimination of drugs from the planet
   ☾ 12-step programs for kids hooked on phonics

◎

☽ great strides in the technology to make things smaller and smaller
   ☾ pocket-size nuclear weapons made in Japan

◎

☽ sports will become less of a business and more of a game again
   ☾ people will still believe that wrestling is real

◎

☽ everyone lives within their income
   ☾ polygamy will be practiced because a third paycheck will be necessary to make ends meet

◎

☽ face-lifts become unnecessary
   ☾ millions of bodies will be silicone from the knees up

67

☻ an end to mall loiterers
☻ mall security guards to be issued stun guns

◎

☻ people are required to take responsibility for their actions
☻ everyone will use victimization as an excuse for their atrocious behavior

◎

☻ safe ATM cubicles
☻ all ATMs will be built inside police stations

◎

☻ good news on the nightly news programs
☻ you'll watch news shows for entertainment, and vice versa

◎

☻ underwear that keeps its shape and stretch
☻ humanity still awaits the development of wedgie-proof underwear

◎

☻ zero inflation
☻ due to linguistic deflation, a picture will be worth only about 500 words

68

😃 carpets that can't be stained

😠 you'll still have to vacuum your flying carpet

◎

😃 driving a car becomes as safe as flying

😠 personal-flight vehicles (flying cars and carpets) will clog up the skies

◎

😃 return of the Sears catalog

😠 stock prices of toilet-tissue companies to plummet

◎

😃 the stock market/Dow Jones Average will be above 6000

😠 financial experts will be outperformed by chimps tossing darts at the newspaper

◎

😃 chemicals will be removed from all cosmetics

😠 liver spots will be in

◎

😃 watches register time beamed from central stations

😠 your pager-watch will let the boss call you anytime

🌑 learning from history

> 🔥 debates over Vietnam will rage on well into the 21st century

◎

🌑 an efficient US Postal Service

> 🔥 the new postal service will be modeled after the DMV

◎

🌑 childhood is still a time of innocence

> 🔥 few kids will ask, "Where do babies come from?"

◎

🌑 air pollution is controlled

> 🔥 kids will ask, "Daddy, why is the sky brown?"

◎

🌑 obedience school required for dogs

> 🔥 still no obedience schools for cats

◎

🌑 something that keeps you from wanting caffeine, sugar, salt, and alcohol

> 🔥 death will be the ultimate rehab program

☽ hairdressers who are taught to do hair the customer's way
   ☽ you'll be able to send out your hair to
   get it done

◎

☽ things don't get worse before they get better
   ☽ Murphy's Law will not be repealed

◎

☽ opening up time capsules all over the world in 2000
   ☽ people in 2000 scratching their heads, wondering
   what was the deal with the pet rock

◎

☽ a talking translator machine for visits to foreign countries
   ☽ translator devices will speak very loudly to help
   foreigners understand

◎

☽ people learn that if it works, don't fix it
   ☽ people never learn that just because
   something works, it doesn't mean you
   should stop improving it

71

☻ being able to study for a test while you sleep

>☹ dreams in which you're late for a test will be more frequent

◎

☻ errorless fax machines

>☹ no one invents a "singing fax machine" to replace the singing telegram

◎

☻ cameras that say "smile" and "say cheese"

>☹ copy machines that say "It's not my fault" when they break down

◎

☻ the animal rights movement succeeds

>☹ you won't be allowed to ride horses or elephants anymore

◎

☻ job security for good workers

>☹ trillions of temps with no benefits

72

😊 windshields that stay clean
> 🙁 **prescription windshields on luxury cars**

◎

😊 magazines that come without inserted cards
> 🙁 **"niche" magazines with a readership of two (e.g., *The Sheila G. Mermelstein Monthly*)**

◎

😊 wood furniture (especially outdoor) that never splinters
> 🙁 **the veneer of civilization will be wearing mighty thin**

◎

😊 flakeless chalk or modern blackboards for all teachers
> 🙁 **scratch 'n' sniff history textbooks**

◎

😊 reruns on command
> 🙁 **the shows you loved as a kid will seem pretty dumb to you as an adult**

◎

😊 the do-it-yourself craze takes hold
> 🙁 **do-it-yourself Home Vasectomy Kits**

�👁 doctors' offices open early in the morning so you can go
before work

> 👁 medical science still won't have an answer for the
> question "Why do men have nipples?"

◎

👁 computers become more commonly owned than TVs

> 👁 people without an Internet address will be known
> as "the cybernetically homeless"

◎

👁 bookmarks that can't fall out of books

> 👁 the instruction manual for your PC may cause a
> hernia if you lift it

◎

👁 new enclosed environments will allow cities to be built in deserts

> 👁 desert cities called "Hellon Earth," "Home-Sweat-
> Home," "Pleasant Underglass," etc.

◎

👁 everyone will have a portable telephone

> 👁 you won't have a good excuse for not calling your
> mother anymore

😊 hydrogen becomes principal fuel for vehicles that don't use electricity

> **😠 a motorcycle is invented that runs on laughing gas—a Yamahahaha**

◎

😊 video discs replace cassettes

> **😠 by 2010 all your compact discs will succumb to dreaded "laser rot"**

◎

😊 no more Prince Charles

> **😠 King Chuck**

◎

😊 sushi declared unhealthy

> **😠 dog brains become an illicit delicacy**

◎

😊 tasty health food

> **😠 Kelp McMuffin is a big hit**

- fewer check-out people and tellers—more machines that can do everything
  - **clerks will be replaced by machines in 2002; in 2022 customers will begin to notice**

- something that makes plants grow without water and sun
  - **seeds of discontent will germinate without much help**

- the Mafia closes up shop
  - **crime-in-the-streets catches up to white-collar crime-in-the-suites**

- honeymoons are guaranteed good weather
  - **iron-clad guarantees are replaced by plastic-clad guarantees**

- cats and dogs taught to feed themselves
  - **your pets will know which fork to use; your children won't**

☻ dogs taught to walk themselves

☺ children will be given names formerly used for cats and dogs

◎

☻ the *Sesame Street* characters grow up and have children

☺ a tabloid exposes how "Big Bird" got his name

◎

☻ a cure for writer's block

☺ writing software will let anyone become a prolific author (not *good*, just prolific)

◎

☻ men and women finally understand each other

☺ hormones allow men to grow breasts so they'll keep their hands to themselves

◎

☻ nuclear power plants become extinct

☺ almost everyone will pronounce it "nuke-yu-lar"

😋 VDT screens that are good for your eyes
> 😖 **human eyes will evolve into a rectangular shape from staring at all those video screens**

◎

😋 banking by phone or computer, the bank line becomes obsolete
> 😖 **phaser-blasting of check writers in the supermarket express lane will be prohibited**

◎

😋 an end to being put on hold
> 😖 **911 will have voice mail ("If you're a victim, press '1' and begin screaming *now . . .*")**

◎

😋 the first garden on Mars
> 😖 **every Martian gardener will have a little green thumb**

◎

😋 agricultural workers are paid well
> 😖 **the minimum wage will be abolished**

78

☙ the abominable snowman is found

> ☙ a UFO lands and is found to be actually *fuzzy,* explaining all those blurry photographs

◎

☙ the Loch Ness monster comes ashore and is friendly

> ☙ Michael Jackson will buy Nessy and have it stuffed

◎

☙ hope is never abandoned

> ☙ the slogan for the future: "Abandon hope all ye who enter here"

◎

☙ the chance to go into the future

> ☙ the 21st century will be a party that most of us will have to leave early

◎

☙ one-of-a-kind items will be inexpensively designed and manufactured

> ☙ everyone on the block will have what everyone else on the block has

79

🌙 large numbers of people will be involved in decision making
> ☄ **with many decision-makers involved, it will be impossible to reach consensus**

◎

🌙 a reduction in excessive materialism
> ☄ **there will be competition to have the least**

◎

🌙 many food additives are banned
> ☄ **everything will taste like bean curd**

◎

🌙 college lecture system replaced by interactive computer teaching
> ☄ **an android becomes president of Yale**

◎

🌙 newspaper boxes where you pay by debit card
> ☄ **the ultimate low will occur when a newspaper machine rejects your debit card for "lack of funds"**

◎

🌙 telephones on which you don't have to dial "9" to get out
> ☄ **you'll have to enter 18 phone access codes to "get in"**

🌣 computer instruction in your home

> 🦜 PC-class-at-home will let you look like a fool in front of your kids

◎

🌣 a message on your in-car computer that tells you where traffic is bad when you punch in the destination

> 🦜 thanks to in-car traffic computers, you'll get p*ssed off even *before* you leave your garage

◎

🌣 being able to learn a language while you sleep

> 🦜 everyone is trilingual but sleeps 15 hours a day

◎

🌣 a laser saw that's accurate and easy to use

> 🦜 a laser-beam nose-hair trimmer that works but occasionally performs lobotomies

◎

🌣 showers that turn off after five minutes

> 🦜 after five minutes your shower will switch from fresh water to funky used "gray water"

81

☽ body odor is cured

☽ laws against "secondhand scents": perfume, B.O., bad breath, etc.

◎

☽ grocery shopping via computer

☽ virtual-shopping program starts with your car circling a 3-D parking lot for an hour

◎

☽ shoe soles that don't mark up floors

☽ scientists invent a drinking glass that doesn't leave a ring—the square glass

◎

☽ drugs off the planet

☽ illegal drug traffic in outer space

◎

☽ tests that prevent people from becoming parents if they're not qualified

☽ you'll have your parenting license suspended if your kid flunks preschool

82

� national health insurance
>☜ **aging boomers will overload all health care facilities**

◎

� meditation taught in schools
>☜ **target practice on playgrounds**

◎

� free movie headsets on airplanes
>☜ **trying to hold a conversation while traveling faster than the speed of sound will be a pain**

◎

� kids in need of work will teach others to read, eliminating illiteracy
>☜ **old classrooms won't have enough electric outlets to plug into the info highway**

◎

� homes built that are burglarproof
>☜ **homes full of radon gas will keep everyone away**

😈 chauffeur services for kids and errand services for parents
> **😈 going outdoors will entail running a gauntlet of mendicants**

◎

😈 options of what to listen to while on hold
> **😈 you'll have to watch Muzak videos or ads while on video-phone hold**

◎

😈 first aid as a required course in school
> **😈 Treating Gunshot Wounds 101**

◎

😈 censoring violence on television
> **😈 Bugs Bunny cartoons will be only 30 seconds long after all the "violence" is cut out**

◎

😈 free continuing education past college
> **😈 perpetual students will stay in school past age 40**

😊 free books for the poor
> 😈 "free" books on tape will come with advertising and a laugh track

◎

😊 a limit on lawyers' and doctors' fees
> 😈 salary caps on everyday occupations

◎

😊 a virtual library in every town
> 😈 libraries will be virtually empty as everyone stays home, "cocooning" in home theaters

◎

😊 cars that don't break down
> 😈 there will be "maintenance-free" cars;
> i.e., when they break, they can't be fixed

◎

😊 gas that can be re-used
> 😈 a way found to collect and recycle livestock flatulence, but no one to do it

☺ bun packages that match hot dog and hamburger packages in number

> ☹ meatless hot dogs won't pass muster

◎

☺ bicycle "pools" to work or school

> ☹ like some sort of nomadic bird, you'll work out of a mobile "nest"

◎

☺ car radios/stereos that automatically lower their volume when a window is opened

> ☹ ultraloud stereos in passing cars will blow away some of your bodily hair

◎

☺ safe places for kids to hang out

> ☹ to look younger, you'll start hanging out with older people

◎

☺ doors that automatically lock upon command

> ☹ the doors to your home will have humongous vault-like locks

❤ the information highway replaces regular highways as the way to commute

> **PCs will be made a tad *too* easy to use, causing a flood of morons to invade cyberspace**

◎

❤ healthy lunches served at schools

> **Burger Kings will be built inside school lunchrooms**

◎

❤ a rosy world economy

> **no tax on optimism, yet**

◎

❤ dress codes in schools—as businesses have

> **further attempts to squelch individuality and self-expression**

◎

❤ humor allowed in school

> **the funniest kids will still be stigmatized as the "class clowns"**

87

😋 a TV system that allows you to watch shows when you want—not according to a schedule

> 😬 **shock therapy for channel zappers**

◎

😋 human cloning

> 😬 **first clones will be named "Gene" and "Xerox"**

◎

😋 Barney becomes extinct

> 😬 ***Barney: The Movie***

◎

😋 rap music goes out of style

> 😬 **you'll hear instrumental versions of rap songs in elevators**

◎

😋 gentle dentists

> 😬 **you'll still have all your teeth, but they'll be in a glass on your nightstand**

88

☽ X rays at airports that don't require putting everything on a conveyor belt

> ☆ airport X rays will check your body for hidden drugs, your lungs for TB, and charge your medical insurance automatically

◎

☽ sports going back to being a game instead of a business

> ☆ athletes never go back to being just jocks, instead of "heroes" and role models

◎

☽ Ross Perot retires from public life

> ☆ Bill Gates buys the earth, renames it "World for Windows"

◎

☽ truly long-lasting light bulbs

> ☆ a bulb that lasts 100 years *will* be invented, but lamps cease working after 3 months

☙ religion is recognized as something personal

    ☙ die-hard fans will form quasi-religious cults around home-shopping shows

◎

☙ replacement of all TV talk shows with educational programming

    ☙ test patterns will get higher ratings than educational shows

◎

☙ free parking everywhere

    ☙ every car will have a counterfeit "handicapped" permit

◎

☙ holidays without traffic fatalities

    ☙ an admission fee will be charged to gawk at car wrecks

◎

☙ machines that shut themselves off

    ☙ you'll go crazy trying to turn off your Perpetual Motion Machine

☯ live video pictures sent to and from your interactive PC
> **☯ the prospect of actually seeing the geeks who write on computer bulletin boards**

◎

☯ science finds way to go faster than the speed of light
> **☯ science never finds way to slow down the speed of time**

◎

☯ roofs that last as long as the house
> **☯ assorted space junk will crash through your roof**

◎

☯ street signs on every corner
> **☯ all street names will be replaced by bland numbers (e.g., Maple Street becomes Street 230221)**

◎

☯ human-friendly insecticides
> **☯ mutant cockroaches as big as poodles**

☻ educators who are good teachers
   🔥 **30th-year high school reunions**

◉

☻ water beds that don't leak
   🔥 **beer-filled beds for people who want a foam mattress**

◉

☻ reasonable prices for hospital care
   🔥 **aspirins for twenty bucks apiece**

◉

☻ a way to save old trees
   🔥 **an upswing in illiteracy will mean fewer books are printed**

◉

☻ videotaped memories of youth to savor in old age
   🔥 **traumatizing tapes of their birth, first potty experiences, etc., will come back to haunt millions of people**

◉

☻ leaf dissolvers for eaves and gutters
   🔥 **leafy trees will be condemned as polluters**

☺ cold remedies that cure rather than just mask symptoms

☹ **cold cure will devastate the pharmaceuticals industry, cause stock market crash**

◎

☺ the return of welcoming parties for new neighbors

☹ **houses with electrified barbed-wire fences are the norm**

◎

☺ better methods to stop bleeding

☹ **Band-Aids continue to be sold in only one flesh color**

◎

☺ T-shirts that don't shrink

☹ **people will advertise their Internet addresses, marital status, etc., on T-shirts**

◎

☺ a cure for migraine headaches

☹ **miraculous cures for horrible diseases, but no cure for hiccups**

☻ relationship education combined with sex education
> ☹ robo-hookers

◎

☻ pianos and guitars that stay in tune
> ☹ it will take no talent to play digital music synthesizers, and it will sound like it

◎

☻ homemakers get respect
> ☹ homemakers get respect, no pay

◎

☻ paint that doesn't fade
> ☹ all your old faxes will fade away

◎

☻ the presidential campaign is limited to four months (July–October)
> ☹ not even Mother Theresa will be squeaky-clean enough to run for president

◎

☻ a qualifying exam for politicians
> ☹ anyone wanting to enter politics is required to have head examined

94

bathroom mirrors/lighting that make you look good
> **bathroom video screen/mirror will replay a tape of someone whose face looks more agreeable in the morning**

◎

when the cable TV goes out, still having network TV
> **cable TV companies enter the phone business and provide the same fine level of service they're famous for**

◎

students taught shorthand for taking better notes
> **spell-checker abuse causes students' spelling scores to nose-dive**

◎

finding a perfect punishment for harassment
> **smiling at a coworker will be considered harassment**

◎

nonitchy wool
> **wool shearing banned as sheep abuse**

☼ fingerprints replace PIN numbers

> ☇ **crimes involving amputated fingers common**

◎

☼ everyone wired into the global village

> ☇ **your business card will be imprinted with your phone, pager, and fax numbers; ID codes for on-line services; Internet address; etc.**

◎

☼ a return to real foods from lite, no cholesterol, low fat

> ☇ **"Einstein-lite" bombs (E=mc) will have half the megatonnage of regular nukes**

◎

☼ computers that know which files you worked on and make copies onto your disk

> ☇ **your office computer will do everything but serve coffee (due to the Mr. Coffee union)**

◎

☼ communities generate energy locally

> ☇ **adolescents' sex drive will be harnessed to power blenders and steel mills**

- a tourists' station will go into operation on the moon
    - **an undertaking service will shoot cremated remains of people and pets into orbit**

- a world lingua franca will be taught in schools
    - **kids will learn 10 languages but will have nothing to say in any of them**

- California breaks off and becomes an island state
    - **in addition to its culture, California will export its smog, gangs, crime, morals, and traffic to the rest of the country**

- the end of international warfare
    - **a civil war erupts between the West Coast and the East Coast**

- cable TV in all households
    - **cable TV in all classrooms**

☻ teaching decision making and thinking

> ☹ **youth-obsessed boomers will need to take classes in How to Be a Geezer**

◉

☻ free electrical system checks by electricians

> ☹ **electric companies will cover up proof that electric power is hazardous to health**

◉

☻ toothpaste that prevents all cavities

> ☹ **the dental lobby will ensure that cavity cures never get on the market**

◉

☻ companies that require you to take an hour off for daily recreation

> ☹ **the tobacco companies get those pesky health warnings off cigarette packs**

◉

☻ cupholders, CD players, and hands-free telephones in all new cars

> ☹ **new cars built so that they can't go faster than 55 mph**

☽ cars that stay cool inside, even in the sun
> ☀ **solar-powered cars that get stranded on cloudy days**

◎

☽ barter replaces currency in many locations
> ☀ **the streets will be littered with discarded, virtually useless pennies**

◎

☽ automated "agents" will scour the Internet searching for jobs for you
> ☀ **your computer agent will want 20% of your salary**

◎

☽ nerds admit they're nerds
> ☀ **the nerds you laugh at today will be the people you work for in the 2000's**

◎

☽ no more punk music
> ☀ **punk songs will be recycled into even more annoying advertising jingles**

99

☺ no ugly people are born
      ☹ **beasts prohibited from marrying beauties**

◎

☺ interplanetary expeditions and commerce
      ☹ **so-called Miss Universe contest still won't have entrants from other planets**

◎

☺ war eliminated
      ☹ **the Third World War will absolutely be the last**

◎

☺ subterranean cities with speedy transport everywhere
      ☹ **no one thinks of building underground trailer parks in the hurricane states**

◎

☺ transcontinental subways
      ☹ **New York subway fare will be raised to $10 to keep out the riffraff**

◎

☺ electric meters read without the services of meter readers
      ☹ **pollsters and market researchers will always be trying to read your mind**

100

people are able to call home and remotely control appliances
or systems

> people too dumb to program their VCRs will
> burn down their houses trying to use remote-
> controlled ovens

◎

any information requested on a computer is available

> asking a PC "What is the meaning of life?"
> will not compute

◎

electrical stimulation of regenerative growth will replace
transplants, implants, and replacement surgery

> entirely new people will be built from the
> stuff cut off during cosmetic surgery

◎

we relearn cooperation, simplicity, and tender loving care

> the phrase "It's so nice to be nice" is subliminally
> burned into our brains

101

☉ competition basically replaced by cooperation
> **even more contests in kite flying, bubble-blowing, etc.**

◎

☉ first humans land on Mars
> **due to the astronomical cost of space travel, any *Starship Enterprise* won't boldly go much farther than Mars**

◎

☉ the greenhouse effect is halted
> **by the time the greenhouse effect stops, we'll all be medium-rare**

◎

☉ telecommunications reduce the need for business travel
> **you'll toil in dehumanized "virtual workplaces"**

◎

☉ a male contraceptive will be available
> **to kill female libido, all that men will have to do is wear short pants and socks that expose a patch of hairy skin below their trouser cuff**

☺ a general understanding of how everything touches and involves everything else prevails

☹ **it becomes politically incorrect to hug**

◎

☺ the return of spirituality

☹ **people "getting religion" all of a sudden**

◎

☺ a way to block sound—for example, of other restaurant patrons—is invented

☹ **people wearing virtual reality gear will become oblivious to every other living thing**

◎

☺ computers that learn

☹ **the first computer to attain human-level understanding will switch itself off**

◎

☺ paid educational sabbaticals offered by corporations

☹ **Cyberpunks Anonymous will treat people for addictions to on-line computer services**

103

☽ the history of the earth in the first billion years will finally be learned

> **☽ it will dawn on people that there is no future, just the past on endless replay**

◎

☽ a national service that moves people if they can get a job and housing elsewhere

> **☽ the unemployed will be frozen until a suitable job opens up, then thawed out**

◎

☽ end-of-the-millennium parties on December 31, 1999

> **☽ nitpicky anal-retentives who won't celebrate the new millennium until January 1, 2001**

◎

☽ a dishwasher that really cleans

> **☽ a dishwashing machine that also puts the dishes _away_ still decades off**

☯ quiet, small aircraft

> ☯ ubiquitous advertising blimps clotting up the sky

◎

☯ books become more popular than TV

> ☯ books-on-videotape succeed because you won't have to visualize anything in your mind's eye

◎

☯ all taxes are filed through a computer accountant

> ☯ scrupulously accurate tax-filing computers will be the Edsel of the future

◎

☯ the country rediscovering Mom-and-Pop businesses

> ☯ "Mom & Pops R Us Co., Inc." becomes a nationwide chain conglomerate, buys out Target and Wal-Mart

◎

☯ growth of cross-cultural cuisine

> ☯ Chinese-German food will make you hungry for power an hour later

🌢 telephone companies do the services of answering machines, which become extinct

> 👁 **answering machines will be able to put you on hold**

◎

🌢 no more general company personnel departments to screen applicants

> 👁 **all job interviewers to employ lie detectors, handwriting analysts, and aura readers**

◎

🌢 an end to loiterers

> 👁 **eject buttons on every street corner**

◎

🌢 computers accepted as expert professional consultants

> 👁 **computer consultants will show you how to ruin your business as well as any human consultant can**

◎

🌢 human brains can control artificial limbs

> 👁 **human brains still can't control reproductive organs**

☾ phaseout of global imbalances in wealth
> **☀ there will be "info-haves" and "have-nots"**

◉

☾ orbital cruises
> **☀ a trip to the nearest star will entail eating airline food and watching the same movies for 10 years**

◉

☾ there are lots of short, great basketball players in the NBA
> **☀ nine-foot-tall genetic freaks will be playing basketball**

◉

☾ much shorter workweeks
> **☀ Wednesday to be eliminated because it's too hard to spell**

◉

☾ utility lines put underground
> **☀ due to land shortages you'll be buried standing up**

🌙 devices will keep children and pets from getting lost or kidnapped

> **it will be discovered that socks lost in washing machines actually enter a 4th dimension**

🌙 homes will be made with completely weatherproof and insulated materials

> **home bulletproofing will be common**

🌙 Fidel Castro will wither and fade away

> **blues music will die as more musicians are prescribed Prozac**

🌙 30th anniversary of Woodstock

> **Woodstock III to reunite Millie and Vanilli**

🌙 menstruation as an option

> **circumcision procedures not at the cutting edge of technology**

108

☙ being able to design your own clothes and accessories and have them custom-made

> ✣ **"Big & Freakish Shops" sell clothing to people with genetic mutations**

◎

☙ direct-speech communication replaces the computer keyboard

> ✣ **it will be impossible to find a typewriter to fill out forms or address envelopes**

◎

☙ TV/VCRs that automatically record your show if you fall asleep

> ✣ **with Smell-o-Vision you'll have to go channel-sniffing instead of channel-surfing**

◎

☙ there will be booths for cellular telephone users

> ✣ **armies of walky-talky pedestrians on their cellular phones**

◎

☙ huge hotels outlawed

> ✣ **at the Star Trek Hotel & Casino in Vegas you'll lose money at warp speed**

109

The Optimist's /Pessimist's Guide to the Millennium

☻ electronic garbage cans that destroy waste
> **☹ irresistible new junk foods that destroy your waist**

◎

☻ being able to try out certain products before you purchase
them
> **☹ family-values laws will prohibit couples from living together before marriage**

◎

☻ prescriptions delivered to your home (like the old days)
> **☹ people will actually refer to the 20th century as "the good old days"**

◎

☻ no more Smurfs or Care Bears
> **☹ the performer formerly known as Prince is still around**

◎

☻ Madonna retires
> **☹ Madonna conceives**

� misery no longer loves company
   😀 **support groups for every conceivable human condition**

◎

😌 cholesterol being found to be good
   😀 **a new health snack, *Lard-on-a-Stick***

◎

😌 a computer "guru" that helps you make tough decisions
   😀 **trying to sue a machine that gives you bad advice will be pretty futile**

◎

😌 useful advice from Dear Abby or Ann Landers
   😀 **people who can write glowing obituaries will be in great demand**

◎

😌 fast coffeemakers
   😀 **vending machine cappuccino**

111

☙ the wealthy being required to give a percentage to charity, not more to the government

> **the government will still steal from the poor and give to the rich**

◎

☙ electronic democracy promoting swift social reform

> **the pace of social change will move slower than a mailman in a coma**

◎

☙ a cure for nail biting

> **no cure for backbiting**

◎

☙ cats become man's best friend

> **dogs devolve back into wolves**

◎

☙ all reference books revised every year

> **reference books inaccurate the moment they're printed**

◎

☙ the abolishment of built-in obsolescence

> **term-limit laws for politicians never enacted**

☻ improved environmental quality
> 🐦 the Bluebird of Happiness will be an
> endangered species

◎

☻ water pollution under control
> 🐦 not as many rivers will burst into flame as before

◎

☻ death penalty abolished
> 🐦 New York to change method of execution from
> lethal injection to a stroll in Central Park

◎

☻ everyone telling the truth all the time
> 🐦 telephones will have built-in B.S. meters

◎

☻ no more chemical dump sites
> 🐦 500 tons of garbage will be generated at the 30th-
> anniversary celebration of Earth Day

113

- public servants who genuinely serve
  - **shooting sprees by disgruntled civil servants are so frequent they're no longer newsworthy**

- an electronic whole-house vacuum so you never have to dust
  - **gigantic "Hoverin' Hoovers" capable of swallowing entire armies will sweep battlefields**

- sunglasses that can change all the way back to no-tint eyeglasses
  - **sunglasses that let you look at an atomic blast from three feet without harming your eyes**

- the three R's are back in demand
  - **no one under 30 will be admitted into new hyper-violent "RRR-rated" movies**

- local theater groups experience a Renaissance
  - **Broadway will be crawling with Disney plays**

☯ fish are tested for toxins before being sold to consumers
> **☯ fish will be so mercury laden you can use them to take your temperature**

◎

☯ people enjoy going to hear live orchestras
> **☯ the "Big Bands" finally make good on their oft-threatened comeback**

◎

☯ the fear of losing jobs to computers doesn't pan out
> **☯ a cheap, low-powered PC will do your job ten times better and faster**

◎

☯ sunglasses that relieve squinting
> **☯ pessimists looking at the future through morose-colored glasses**

◎

☯ completely safe and convenient baggage check at airports
> **☯ your bags will be whisked at supersonic speeds to the wrong airport**

- gardening replaces agriculture as the major form of food production
  - **bionic Chia Pets are playful edible pets, but will shed grass all over your house**

- paperwork is reduced in every field
  - **the concept of the "paperless office" will look good only on paper**

- high-tech direct satellite broadcasts to a small dish in your home
  - **you'll discover your DBS satellite dish works better with a coat hanger wrapped around it**

- the beginning of a federation of the whole of humanity
  - **the world will consist of 1,000 mono-ethnic countries, all of whom can't stand each other**

- all bank robbers get caught
  - **computer-literate mobsters to commit info-highway robbery**

☻ police departments to rely more on computerized
crime solvers

> ☻ you'll start to notice how *young* all the
> police officers look

◎

☻ people don't have the time or reasons to commit crimes

> ☻ just thinking of a crime will be tantamount
> to committing it

◎

☻ scientists discover an organism that cleans up oil spills quickly
and then self-destructs

> ☻ as a result of massive oil spills, tuna will be sold
> leaded or unleaded

◎

☻ people never get out of shape

> ☻ people stay in shape, but the shape will be that of
> a clothes hamper

117

☽ though you'll be 60 on the outside, you'll still feel 16 on the inside

> ☼ **cars your age will be nothing but broken-down rusting hulks**

◎

☽ hockey games without fights

> ☼ **hockey games without fights**

◎

☽ a high probability that things will actually get better

> ☼ **a small probability of having a president named "Newt"**

◎

☽ people enjoy the thought of reincarnation

> ☼ **numerous *Guides to the Afterlife* to be published**

◎

☽ "classics" movie channels dedicated to presenting simple entertainment

> ☼ ***Casablanca* and other film classics will be re-reviewed and declared "over-rated"**

118

☻ high-definition TV becomes reality

☹ **broadcasters will switch to HDTV the day after you plunk down big bucks for an "old standard" TV**

◎

☻ a method discovered to prevent earthquakes

☹ **a method discovered to start earthquakes: every person in China stomps feet simultaneously**

◎

☻ college sports will become deprofessionalized

☹ **Buffalo loses 25th straight Super Bowl**

◎

☻ ERA finally passed

☹ **women go on a sex strike until ERA is passed**

◎

☻ passports in which you can be identified in some way other than a picture

☹ **you won't get "carded" at bars anymore**

☺ when McDonald's does it "your way"
☹ audio-animatronic Frank Sinatras singing "My Way"

◉

☺ being able to try on clothes electronically without actually changing into them
☹ low-tech clothing stores will just use fun-house mirrors to make you look skinny

◉

☺ instructions only in your language
☹ ATMs with instructions in 27 languages

◉

☺ the big guys don't always win
☹ "less is more" never unseats "bigger is better"

◉

☺ simple ideas worded in uncomplicated ways
☹ "no" still incomprehensible to many

◉

☺ babies stop crying when phones ring and when out in public
☹ it will be an FAA regulation that you sit within 10 feet of a screaming infant on all airplanes

120

😊 neurosis declared a communicable disease

☹ **ulcers found to be hereditary—you get them from your kids**

◎

😊 a gauge that tells how many more miles you can go on the gas you have

☹ **from genetic analysis, you'll know how much longer you have to live**

◎

😊 parochial schoolteachers will get paid what public schoolteachers do

☹ **rehab centers that treat former students of parochial schools for psychological and ruler-inflicted scars**

◎

😊 people learn to work with pressure

☹ **people who were in really bad moods during the '90s finally explode**

121

☺ figuring out the Internet
>☹ **wasting hours exchanging trivial gossip with faceless strangers over an electronic back fence**

◎

☺ tennis balls that roll back onto your court
>☹ **perverse bowling balls with collision-avoidance radar**

◎

☺ each seaside community has a community yacht
>☹ **flotillas of rich "yacht people" will flee the United States and its taxes**

◎

☺ people keeping their expectations to themselves
>☹ **people in former superpowers dealing with a life of lowered expectations**

◎

☺ completely safe fireworks displays
>☹ **you'll spend the Fourth of July watching computer-simulated fireworks on a tiny view-screen**

� 1984 came and went and Big Brother was not watching
☟ **George Orwell was off by 16 years**

◎

☟ newspapers start replacing their bad news with good
☟ **newspaper with nothing but "factoids" debuts (oops, sorry—we already have *USA Today*)**

◎

☟ phrases like "politically correct" and "reaching closure" are unpopular
☟ **people will say "I'm evolving on this issue" when they mean they don't know**

◎

☟ the countries of the world agree on ethical standards for science and technology
☟ **"morality engineers" will tinker with your conscience**

◎

☟ worry-remover medicine
☟ **alcohol remains legal, pot's not**

☙ a lightbulb that can be adjusted to any wattage
> ☙ **when a cartoon character gets a good idea, an LED will light up over its head**

◎

☙ toys with homing devices so you can find them
> ☙ **a "cloaking device" that you'll keep losing**

◎

☙ scuffless shoes
> ☙ **electric elevator shoes for people with occasional low self-esteem**

◎

☙ guaranteed untainted meat and dairy products
> ☙ **candidates for political office with untainted pasts will be in very short supply**

◎

☙ something better that replaces the ladder
> ☙ **out-of-work "Human Pyramids" from circuses will rent themselves as ladder substitutes**

◎

☙ *Cats* leaves Broadway
> ☙ **new Broadway hit, *Dogs!***

124

☻ community theaters spring up again
> ☹ goatee-sporting neo-beatniks reading bad poetry in Starbucks cafes

◎

☻ affordable is the rule, not the exception
> ☹ your children will have to assume your home's 50-year mortgage

◎

☻ Isaac Asimov books go out of print
> ☹ King's Books will be stores that sell only Stephen King books

◎

☻ the taste of liver and onions is improved
> ☹ someone invents liver-and-onion-flavored toothpaste

◎

☻ there are no more assault guns on Earth
> ☹ ban on assault weapons will be repealed

☻ more bargain-book sections in bookstores
>☹ the "Occult" section in bookstores will now be called "New Age"

◎

☻ Manhattan apartments must be of minimum size and affordably priced
>☹ closet-size apartments in Manhattan are readily available to any and all millionaires

◎

☻ the Infomercial Network is extremely popular, providing a channel where you can watch commercials if and when you want to
>☹ ex-MTV VJs will host tacky infomercials

◎

☻ punishment will fit the crime
>☹ "eye-for-an-eye law" to hit a snag in the case of a killer-cannibal

◎

☻ technology makes Earth a prettier place
>☹ "Walkie-Watchies"—people walking around wearing satellite-dish beanies and video-visor helmets on their heads

☽ on-line services charge really minimal fees
> ☀ **Microsoft's on-line service will swallow up all other services and become a monopoly**

◎

☽ a single format for personal computers
> ☀ **a holy war will erupt between IBM and Mac users, unleashing killer viruses that erase millions of memories**

◎

☽ people become less attracted to horror stories and thrillers
> ☀ ***A Clockwork Orange* will seem like a fable of a kinder, gentler time**

◎

☽ *Star Trek* is still on TV and in the movies
> ☀ ***Star Trek: The Tenth Generation* makes its debut on TV and *The Really, REALLY Last Voyage III* opens in theaters (in which William Shatner's hairpiece comes back as a Tribble)**

127

🌢 glues and other everyday products no longer contain any intoxicants

> **🐦 sucking poison gases from smoldering vegetables through paper tubes is still amazingly popular**

◎

🌢 meanness lessens as acceptance increases

> **🐦 meanness and dumbness are the Zeitgeist**

◎

🌢 natural foods and cosmetics become less foreign

> **🐦 weird unguents in use: udder balm, tiger ointment, horse-hair shampoo**

◎

🌢 movie cineplexes are limited to eight theaters

> **🐦 home theaters drive public theaters out of business**

◎

🌢 health clubs are extremely popular

> **🐦 health clubs and churches merge, offering power-prayer, low-impact genuflecting, and aerobic rosaries**

128

☽ solar-powered buildings
> **☽ self-esteem–powered narcissists**

◎

☽ an electronic Utopia
> **☽ Huxley's *Brave New World***

◎

☽ virtual reality for the world's great structures and places
> **☽ museums will be built inside the homes of the
> wealthy, inaccessible to the public**

◎

☽ "abracadabra" really works
> **☽ personal canisters of pepper-spray do the job
> formerly done by the police**

◎

☽ afternoon tea becomes important again
> **☽ health zealots crusading against coffee and tea
> addiction**

◎

☽ agility can be taught
> **☽ the "klutz-gene" is never isolated**

129

☹ no more baby booms

   ☺ **another baby boom is predicted for the first decade of the new millennium**

◎

☹ peace on Earth

   ☺ **cataclysmic wobbling of Earth to occur when all the planets align on May 5, 2000**

◎

☹ street mimes outlawed

   ☺ **accordion playing anywhere in this universe not banned yet**

◎

☹ passenger rides to the moon

   ☺ **the moon becomes a new Disney attraction, "Luna Land"**

◎

☹ no product is poorly made

   ☺ **science will have put humans on Mars, but still can't make panty hose that won't run**

130

everyone's taxes are reduced because computers have located all those who were not paying their fair share

> **computer stool pigeons will be found hanging by their power cords**

◎

geometric growth in the number of patents issued to corporate R&D departments

> **the demise of the lone mad inventor who always works in a smoke-filled basement**

◎

more people doing yoga and meditation than drugs

> **stargazing replaced by navelgazing**

◎

we communicate with other life forms in space and find they are friendly

> **remember that *Twilight Zone* episode—"To Serve Man" was the title of a COOKBOOK**

131

😊 hearing little bells going off, representing angels getting their wings

> 😦 **millions of hours will be spent trying to prove the existence of angels**

◎

😊 small businesses popping up everywhere—a new breed of entrepreneur with few layers of management

> 😦 **the surfeit of baby boomers jockeying for the few available spaces in senior management**

◎

😊 the prophets of gloom and doom are continually proven wrong

> 😦 **Nostradamus will be considered an optimist**

◎

😊 McDonald's is at least half vegetarian

> 😦 **cows go extinct as Mickey-D's serves 200 billionth burger**

◎

😊 distinctions between generations become fuzzy

> 😦 **the Pepsi Generation switches to Pepto-Bismol**

☙ knowing the answers to almost all of your questions

> ☙ you'll finally have all the answers to life, but nobody will ask you any questions

◎

☙ people respecting their bodies

> ☙ body-piercing fad will become passé after you finally get a nose-ring

◎

☙ government becomes very, very small

> ☙ people will rail against government handouts until their ox gets gored

◎

☙ people power becomes very, very big

> ☙ it will be harder to do things for yourself because you'll be dependent on a slew of technological middlemen

◎

☙ restaurant food is required to be fresh

> ☙ seafood restaurants will be serving only imitation crabmeat

133

😋 tap water is safe and health-giving once again
    😈 bottled water will be labeled with its year, like wine

◎

😋 learning how to spell millennium
    😈 you'll need to know the difference between "prostrate" and "prostate"

◎

😋 the 21st century will bring on the optimism
    😈 "millenniaphobes" will claim that they're allergic to the 21st century

◎

😋 all places take all major credit cards
    😈 sidewalk panhandlers will accept Visa and Mastercard

◎

😋 dark clothing repels lint
    😈 people will have their pets' fur dyed to coordinate with their homes

☻ paint that goes on perfectly and never streaks
☹ polka-dot paint not perfected

◎

☻ personal electronic zappers for flies, etc.
☹ Personal Insect Zapper to be recalled because it still has bugs in it

◎

☻ the Energizer Bunny runs out of energy
☹ interactive TVs won't let you whip out a gun and blow the Energizer Bunny's head off

◎

☻ shoes that stretch as your kids' feet grow
☹ your kids will be growing, growing—gone

◎

☻ flowers that stay good for a month
☹ irradiated vegetables will stay fresh for months and do double duty as night-lights

135

☻ cookbooks with unstainable pages
>☺ *Cooking with Mr. Ed*—a new recipe book for cooking with horse meat

◎

☻ castles are built in the United States
>☺ Wal-Mart castles sold pre-fab

◎

☻ purse exchange services
>☺ cyber scam-artists will take your wallet to the cleaners

◎

☻ snow that can be "ordered" for your lawn
>☺ Perrier to import and sell designer snow for upscale customers

◎

☻ getting used to writing 2000!
>☺ "round-number neurosis" to afflict millions

◎

☻ the chance to start over
>☺ if we don't get it right this millennium, there's always the next one

136

☻ no more face-lifts
> ☹ **Dick Clark will begin to show signs of aging**

◎

☻ technology solves most problems
> ☹ **there'll be multiple snakes in the technological Eden**

◎

☻ strict gun regulations exist, few people are killed by guns
> ☹ **legalized handguns bring back the wild, wild West—and North, and South, and East**

◎

☻ police walk a beat and are very visible, reducing crime
> ☹ **privatized police provide protection to all who can afford them**

◎

☻ young people not struggling to have fun
> ☹ **the young will be walking arsenals of bitterness**

☻ an end to frivolous lawsuits
> ☻ a court will rule that if your ancestor found a 10-dollar bill in the street, the loser's descendants can sue you for the money plus interest

◎

☻ improved infant mortality rates
> ☻ lawsuit-leery doctors will deliver 90% of all babies via C-section

◎

☻ men can become pregnant
> ☻ abortion will become free and unlimited

◎

☻ it will be the best of times if you're an optimist
> ☻ if you're a pessimist it will be the worst of times, and the worst of times

◎

☻ undetectable toupees
> ☻ after you spend a fortune on hair restoration, shaved heads will be declared sexy

☻ schools are a safe place to work and learn

> ☻ **schoolteachers will wear tweed bulletproof vests with elbow patches**

◎

☻ the development of space colonies prevents the accumulation of personal property

> ☻ **people will still strive to have their own "space" in space**

◎

☻ ocean-floor mining by robots

> ☻ **scientists barnacle-proof Robbie the Robot and implant Jacques Cousteau's brain**

◎

☻ America has a balanced budget—a tribute we leave for our children and grandchildren

> ☻ **the dollar will be devalued when the federal debt hits seven trillion dollars in year 2000**

☻ the average car will cost less than $15,000
> 👿 an average car will cost over $30,000—luxury models over $100,000

◎

☻ enjoying each day of one's life
> 👿 having to stare your own mortality in the face

◎

☻ lawyers, by law, must find out the truth above all
> 👿 the EPA won't crack down on lawyers using smoke screens

◎

☻ science fiction is alive and well
> 👿 science fiction will turn its attention to the 22nd century as the hope for the future

◎

☻ schools change their educational philosophy to teaching students how to learn
> 👿 everything a student learns in college will be obsolete in three years

☻ there will be a lie detector test that is 100% accurate

    ☹ **crooks will learn how to study for a lie detector test**

◎

☻ lasers fix tooth decay

    ☹ **people will flash blindingly bright, laser-enhanced smiles**

◎

☻ the silent majority speaks up

    ☹ **the silent majority becomes a violent minority**

◎

☻ reliable chemical tests for mental disorders are introduced

    ☹ **Home Sanity Tests—if you can't pee on the little stick *without* laughing, you're probably OK**

◎

☻ no more OPEC

    ☹ **OPEC will suppress solar power because they can't own sunshine**

141

☕ clocks synchronized to a master atomic clock
☕ "Big Ben" will become a digital clock

◎

☕ no more aerosol sprays exist
☕ "hair-in-a-can" exempted from spray-can ban

◎

☕ regional accents are alive and well
☕ everyone will have that flat "from Nowhere" accent and sound the same

◎

☕ parents teaching values, so there are no juvenile offenders
☕ eleven-year-olds on death row

◎

☕ all sex becomes safe because people are careful and smart
☕ sex in the future will involve full-body latex wet suits, and a pair of tongs

142

☺ all tapes and discs can be dubbed onto one new medium that won't become obsolete

> ☹ **your tape and CD library will be made obsolete by small Memory Cards, then by Music Pills, and so on and so forth . . .**

◎

☺ big city mass transit is clean, efficient, and loved

> ☹ **L.A.'s subway will carry the movers and shakers**

◎

☺ laser-beam shavers keep you clean-shaven for a week

> ☹ **laser-beam shavers still require little bits of tissue paper to stanch the bleeding**

◎

☺ everyone lives for today

> ☹ **future motto: "Today may be the last day of the rest of your life"**

143

🌣 the Social Security system will invest your money so that all
retirees become financially independent

> 🐍 **Generation X will have to pay crushing
> payroll taxes to support retiring boomers
> beginning in 2013**

◉

🌣 the average life expectancy is a healthy 85

> 🐍 **medical science will keep comatose, incapacitated
> humans alive indefinitely, but pets will be
> humanely put to rest**

◉

🌣 pets will not be overbred

> 🐍 **dogs will be overbred into bizarre, sickly living
> toys that bear little resemblance to Lassie**

◉

🌣 astronomical delights

> 🐍 **for all those who missed seeing Halley's Comet
> last time, you'll get another chance in 2061**

☽ culture hitting new heights
> ☙ **the nadir of popular culture will sink to lower-than-Hitler-in-hell levels**

◎

☽ beef will be safe but not in great demand
> ☙ **beef will be so pricy, chuck chop will be renamed "Charles Chop"**

◎

☽ the gene that causes Alzheimer's is discovered and a cure follows
> ☙ **Alzheimer's cause will be traced to the aluminum in soft-drink cans**

◎

☽ former presidents continue to make contributions through public service and writings
> ☙ **fanatical listeners of far-right talk-radio shows will make frequent assassination attempts**

◎

☽ Medicare made very simple
> ☙ **your brain will turn to mush trying to unravel the intricacies of Medicare**

145

😋 an end to the search for the Fountain of Youth
> 😏 **lots of Peter Pans in age denial, doing ludicrous things**

◎

😋 living for tomorrow
> 😏 **forgetting to revel in your time**

◎

😋 agents are no longer necessary to succeed
> 😏 **every worker will have an agent, not just writers and actors**

◎

😋 virtual reality is used only in good ways—nothing scary or upsetting
> 😏 **people freaking out from "bad VR trips"**

◎

😋 not having to "learn" to make the most of life
> 😏 **when you've finally learned to make the most of life, most of life will be gone**

146

☻ divorces well under 50%

> ☹ Mattel to introduce new Divorced Barbie—
> she comes with all of Ken's stuff

◎

☻ keeping track of the millennium's interesting and joyful "firsts"

> ☹ you'll still have "firsts" in your life:
> first kidney stone; first little pee squirt
> when you sneeze; etc.

◎

☻ welfare is temporary and more is spent on education

> ☹ less welfare for poor, more entitlements for upper-
> class and corporations

◎

☻ quiet video games

> ☹ five-year-olds will beat you at video games

◎

☻ Uncle Walt Disney was right—"It's a small world after all"

> ☹ Dick Tracy was right—"Whoever controls
> magnetism will control the universe"

☻ a movement to make a much better world for our children and grandchildren

> ☺ you'll feel pretty guilty about the world you're leaving to your kids, but there'll be a pill for that, too

◎

☻ Gary Larson and the *Far Side* unretires

> ☺ *Far Side* desk calendars for the next thousand years

◎

☻ it is considered cool to be intelligent

> ☺ scientists will never lose their popular image as evil mad-scientist Dr. Frankensteins

◎

☻ looking at the countdown clock and realizing you still have time to make a contribution

> ☺ you'll begin to have the feeling that your days are numbered

148

☻ faithful employees are trusted and appreciated

> ☹ **you'll be watched constantly on surveillance cameras while you work**

◉

☻ *America's Funniest* shows end

> ☹ **new combination crime/comedy TV show, *America's Funniest Surveillance Tapes***

◉

☻ schoolchildren will be taught that numbers are tools

> ☹ **innumeracy will be an even bigger problem than illiteracy**

◉

☻ great genius will constitute those who use their heads and hearts

> ☹ **the word "genius" continues to be used fast and loosely, applied to Einstein as well as rock stars**

◉

☻ a new flat tax makes doing taxes a breeze and paying more fair

> ☹ **genetically manipulated Brainiacs with huge foreheads will prepare your taxes**

☻ diets and exercise are "natural"
    ☹ eating meat will be declared immoral

◎

☻ the Muppets are still around
    ☹ puppets will demand to be called
    "handheld persons"

◎

☻ Las Vegas becomes a family-oriented vacation spot
    ☹ Vegas will vie with New York, Los Angeles,
    and Chicago as the largest metropolitan area
    in United States

◎

☻ the greenhouse effect is reversed
    ☹ greenhouse effect envelopes the earth in
    mushrooms and toadstools

◎

☻ refrigerators no longer use harmful chemicals
    ☹ refrigerators unnecessary after the coming
    Ice Age

150

🌣 every imaginable store will have catalog shopping and home delivery

> **🙂 Kmart to sell "Blue-Light Special" beer, and Sears will provide psychotherapy**

◎

🌣 children and adults loving each other unconditionally

> **🙂 the distinction between adult and child to blur**

◎

🌣 parents stop nagging about maturity

> **🙂 an inherently immature generation in its second childhood**

◎

🌣 people less impressed by the rich and famous

> **🙂 people will spend big bucks on "celebrity relics"**

◎

🌣 centennial commemorations of key 1900 events

> **🙂 silly celebrations of Spencer Tracy's 100th birthday**

😊 no more stickers on fruits and vegetables

    😟 **all fruit and cheese will come wrapped in smell proof plastic**

◎

😊 saving consistently and at an early age for your retirement

    😟 **look forward to having spine-tingling discussions about your pension plan**

◎

😊 senior citizens are welcomed, not ignored

    😟 **by 2030 the United States will have twice as many senior citizens as it did in the 1990s**

◎

😊 no regrets

    😟 **there'll be days when you wish you *had* run away with the circus**

◎

😊 clean energy preventing acid rain and water

    😟 **acrid lakes and streams that will make the Dead Sea seem lively**

152

☽ comedy that has no age barriers
>☾ **younger people won't "get" your jokes anymore**

◎

☽ music composed for the millennium
>☾ **"Also Sprach Zarathustra" (the "2001 theme") will be played *ad nauseam***

◎

☽ computer "ghost writers" will help you write your autobiography
>☾ **"ghost painters" will crank out artwork that you can sign and pass off as your own**

◎

☽ a return to the basics
>☾ **coal-powered computers**

◎

☽ Bob Dole will be given a funny-bone transplant
>☾ **his body will reject it**

153

❁ renewed public interest in the arts and humanities
>	❁ bloody culture wars break out between afficionados of Mozart and fans of The Three Stooges

◎

❁ kids decide gangs are out
>	❁ repealed child-labor laws will keep kids off the streets and out of trouble

◎

❁ we'll be living in the best of all possible worlds
>	❁ you'll fear that the above is true

◎

❁ the future will be an inviting, exciting time
>	❁ it'll be a nice place to visit, but you wouldn't want to live there